MACARTHUR BIBLE STUDIES

EPHESIANS

Our Immeasurable Blessings in Christ

JOHN
MACARTHUR

EPHESIANS
MACARTHUR BIBLE STUDIES

Copyright © 2000, John F. MacArthur, Jr. Published by Word Publishing, P.O.
Box 141000, Nashville, TN 37214. All rights reserved. No portion of this book
may be reproduced, stored in a retrieval system, or transmitted in any form or
by any means—electronic, mechanical, photocopy, recording, or any other—
except for brief quotations in printed reviews, without the prior permission of
the publisher.

Scripture passages taken from:
The Holy Bible, *New King James Version*
Copyright © 1979, 1980, 1982 by Thomas Nelson. All rights reserved.

Cover Art by The Puckett Group.
Interior design and composition by Design Corps, Batavia, IL.

Produced with the assistance of the Livingstone Corporation. Project staff
include Dave Veerman, Christopher D. Hudson, and Amber Rae.

Project editor: Len Woods

ISBN 0-8499-5541-6

All rights reserved. *Printed in the United States of America.*

00 01 02 03 04 PHX 5 6

Table of Contents

EPHESIANS

Introduction

The letter is addressed to the church in the city of Ephesus, capital of the Roman province of Asia (Asia Minor, modern Turkey). Because the name Ephesus is not mentioned in every early manuscript of this letter, some scholars believe the letter was an encyclical, intended to be circulated and read among all the churches in Asia Minor and was simply sent first to believers in Ephesus.

Author and Date

No evidence has arisen for questioning Paul's authorship. He is indicated as author in the opening salutation (1:1; 3:1). Written from prison in Rome (Acts 28:16–31) sometime between A.D. 60–62, the letter is, therefore, often labeled a prison epistle (along with Philippians, Colossians, and Philemon). Ephesians may have been composed almost at the same time as Colossians and initially sent with that epistle and Philemon by Tychicus (6:21–22; Colossians 4:7–8). See Introduction to Philippians: Author and Date in *The MacArthur Study Bible* for a discussion of the city from which Paul wrote.

Background and Setting

The gospel probably was first brought to Ephesus by Priscilla and Aquila, an exceptionally gifted couple (see Acts 18:26) who had been left there by Paul on his second missionary journey (Acts 18:18–19). Located at the mouth of the Cayster River, on the east side of the Aegean Sea, Ephesus was perhaps best known for its magnificent temple of Artemis, or Diana, one of the seven wonders of the ancient world. It was also an important political, educational, and commercial center, ranking with Alexandria in Egypt and Antioch of Pisidia, in southern Asia Minor.

Later, Paul firmly established this fledgling church on his third missionary journey (Acts 19), and he pastored it for some three years. After Paul left, Timothy pastored the congregation for perhaps a year and a half, primarily to counter the false teaching of a few influential men (such as Hymenaeus and Alexander), who were probably elders in the congregation there (1 Timothy 1:3, 20). Because of those men, the church at Ephesus was plagued by "fables and endless genealogies" (1 Timothy 1:4) and by such ascetic and unscriptural ideas as the forbidding of marriage and abstaining from certain foods (1 Timothy 4:3). Although those false teachers did not rightly understand Scripture, they propounded their ungodly interpretations with confidence (1 Timothy 1:7), which produced in the church harmful "disputes rather than godly edification which is in faith" (1 Timothy 1:4). About thirty years later, Christ gave the apostle John a letter for the church indicating that its people had left their first love for Him (Revelation 2:1–7).

Historical and Theological Themes

The first three chapters are theological, emphasizing New Testament doctrine, whereas the last three chapters are practical and focus on Christian behavior. Above all, this is a letter of encouragement and admonition, written to remind believers of their immeasurable blessings in Jesus Christ, not only to be thankful for those blessings, but also to live in a manner worthy of them. Despite, and partly even because of, Christians' great blessings in Jesus Christ, they are sure to be tempted by Satan to self-satisfaction and complacency. Thus, in the last chapter, Paul reminds believers of the full and sufficient spiritual armor supplied to them through God's Word and by His Spirit (6:10–17) and of their need for vigilant and persistent prayer (6:18).

A key theme of Ephesians is the mystery (meaning a heretofore unrevealed truth) of the church—"that the Gentiles should be fellow heirs, of the same body, and partakers of His promise in Christ through the gospel" (3:6), a truth completely hidden from the Old Testament saints (3:5, 9). All believers in Jesus Christ, the Messiah, are equal before the Lord as His children and as citizens of His eternal kingdom, a marvelous truth that only believers of this present age possess. Paul also speaks of the mystery of the church as the bride of Christ (5:32; Revelation 21:9).

Paul emphasizes the major truth that the church is Christ's present spiritual, earthly body, also a distinct and formerly unrevealed truth about God's people. This metaphor depicts the church not as an organization, but as a living organism composed of mutually related and interdependent parts. Christ is Head of the body, and the Holy Spirit is its lifeblood. The body functions through the faithful use of its members' various spiritual gifts, sovereignly and uniquely given by the Holy Spirit to each believer.

Another prominent theme is the riches and fullness of blessing to believers. Paul writes of "the riches of His [God's] grace (1:7), "the unsearchable riches of Christ" (3:8), and "the riches of His glory" (3:16). Paul admonishes believers to "be filled with all the fullness of God" (3:19), to "come to the unity of the faith and of the knowledge of the Son of God, to a perfect man, to the measure of the stature of the fullness of Christ" (4:13), and "to be filled with the Spirit" (5:18). Believers' riches in Christ are based on God's grace (1:2, 6–7; 2:7), peace (1:2), will (1:5), pleasure and purpose (1:9), glory (1:12–14), calling and inheritance (1:18), power and strength (1:19; 6:10), love (2:4), workmanship (2:10), Holy Spirit (3:16), offering and sacrifice (5:2), and armor (6:11–13). The word "riches" is used five times in the letter; "grace" is used twelve times; "glory" eight times, "fullness" or "filled" six times; and the key phrase "in Christ" (or "in Him") twelve times.

The Riches of His Grace

Opening Thought

1) The New Testament repeatedly calls the message of God's offer of grace to sinners through the substitutionary death of Christ the "gospel" or "good news".

When we hear good news, we want to share it spontaneously with everyone we meet. For example, think of getting a raise, finding out you're going to have a baby, and so forth. Yet many believers in Christ are reluctant to communicate their faith with others. They seem complacent about this staggering promise of salvation from sin and death through Christ.

Why is this so?

They don't understand how good the good news is. They don't know how inadequate the other so-called answers in the world are. Don't have a good sense of sin. Fear of reaction of others. Sense of unworthiness. We spend too much time thinking about the things of this world. Lose our first love.

Background of the Passage

Paul had spent three years pastoring the church at Ephesus and instructing them in the things of God. During that time he would have preached and taught all the great truths of this epistle. Because of Satanic opposition as well as the human tendency to forget what is true, however, Paul sensed the need for a letter of reminder and encouragement. He wanted to challenge his brothers and sisters in the faith to grow in grace and to stand firm in the midst of an evil age.

Rather than beginning with a long list of dos and don'ts, Paul began his correspondence with a refresher course in theology, answering questions such as these: How is salvation accomplished? Why did God bestow His grace on us? What does the future hold for those who put their faith in Christ?

Paul recognized that such an emphasis on difficult doctrines was necessary because right God-honoring *behavior* always springs from right *beliefs*. Christians who lack a proper theological foundation will not have a proper appreciation for what God has done, nor will they adequately understand the resources at their disposal in the life of faith.

In the following passage, Paul describes believers' infinite blessings in Christ. Specifically he gives a panoramic view of God's great salvation.

Bible Passage

Read 1:1–14, noting the key words, phrases, and definitions to the right of the passage.

Ephesians 1:1–14

1 *Paul, an apostle of Jesus Christ by the will of God, To the saints who are in Ephesus, and faithful in Christ Jesus:* bound together

2 *Grace to you and peace from God our Father and the Lord Jesus Christ.*

3 *Blessed [be] the God and Father of our Lord Jesus Christ, who has blessed us with every spiritual*

blessed (v. 3)—from the same Greek word as "eulogy," which means to praise or commend. It refers to God's kindness to us as well as the appreciation or thanks we express back to Him.

He chose us (v. 4)—This refers to God's pretemporal, sovereign act of electing who will be saved, a common theme in Paul's writ-

6

blessing in the heavenly [places] in Christ,

4 just as He chose us in Him before the foundation of the world, that we should be holy and without blame before Him in love,

5 having predestined us to adoption as sons by Jesus Christ to Himself, according to the good pleasure of His will,

6 to the praise of the glory of His grace, by which He has made us accepted in the Beloved.

7 In Him we have redemption through His blood, the forgiveness of sins, according to the riches of His grace

8 which He made to abound toward us in all wisdom and prudence,

9 having made known to us the mystery of His will, according to His good pleasure which He purposed in Himself,

10 that in the dispensation of the fullness of the times He might gather together in one all things in Christ, both which are in heaven and which are on earth—in Him.

11 In Him also we have obtained an inheritance, being predestined according to the purpose of Him who works all things according to the counsel of His will,

12 that we who first trusted in Christ should be to the praise of His glory.

13 In Him you also [trusted], after you heard the word of truth, the gospel of your salvation; in whom also, having believed, you were sealed with the Holy Spirit of promise,

14 who is the guarantee of our inheritance until the redemption of the purchased possession, to the praise of His glory.

ings (Romans 8:29; 9:11; 1 Thessalonians 1:3,4; 2 Thessalonians 2:13; 2 Timothy 2:10).

predestined (v. 5)—God's perfect plan for the destiny of His creatures that conforms with His love and grace and with human beings' responsibility to believe in Jesus as Lord and Savior.

adoption as sons (v. 5)—the spiritual act whereby God brings a regenerated believer into His own family (see John 1:12)

redemption (v. 7)—The Greek word means to "buy back" or "ransom." Used in a salvation context, it refers to Christ's death on the cross that paid the price required to purchase the elect from the slave market of sin.

dispensation of the fullness of the times (v. 10)—The Greek word translated "dispensation" is the word from which we get our English word "economy." It means God's perfect arrangement or administration of events and history to accomplish His plan. The phrase here refers to the millennial kingdom at the end of world history.

sealed with the Holy Spirit (v. 13)—The spiritual act in which the Spirit of God, at the time of conversion, indwells a new believer and secures and preserves his or her salvation.

Understanding the Text

2) This passage expresses God's salvation in terms of the past (election, verses 3–6a), the present (redemption, verses 6b-11) and the future (inheritance, vv. 12–14). Why does Paul take such a broad view?

Because his topic is the large purposes, the overall plan of God. He wants to To show the eternal nature. World view The Trinity involved

> Go through the passage and underline the various references to the members of the Trinity and the unique role each played in the salvation process.

3) Several times in these verses we are granted insights into God's purpose(s) for salvation. Why did "God predestine[d] us to adoption as sons . . ." (v. 5)? Verse six says this was done "to the praise of the glory of His grace." What does this mean? How does this fit with the last phrases in verses 12 and 14?

What He does for us and through us reveals His glory - His character, holiness, love, wisdom, etc. Should do it in the present

(verses to consider: Isaiah 43:2; 1 Corinthians 10:31)

> Circle any and all phrases in this passage that speak to the issue of God's motive(s) in salvation.

4) The text states clearly that God receives glory, pleasure, and praise from our salvation. What does Paul say that human objects of salvation receive from the gracious hand of God?

Salvation, redemption, forgiveness - all spiritual blessings in the heavenlies, inheritance, position of sonship. Legal status,

Forgiveness of sins - Humility

Cross-Reference

Read the following passage and consider what Paul has to say about our salvation from sin and its penalty.

Romans 3:21–26

21 *But now the righteousness of God apart from the law is revealed, being witnessed by the Law and the Prophets,*

22 *even the righteousness of God, through faith in Jesus Christ, to all and on all who believe. For there is no difference;*

23 *for all have sinned and fall short of the glory of God,*

24 *being justified freely by His grace through the redemption that is in Christ Jesus,*

25 *whom God set forth [as] a propitiation by His blood, through faith, to demonstrate His righteousness, because in His forbearance God had passed over the sins that were previously committed,*

26 *to demonstrate at the present time His righteousness, that He might be just and the justifier of the one who has faith in Jesus.*

Exploring the Meaning

5) How does 1:7 relate to the passage from Romans quoted above?

We have been redeemed and forgiven through Christ through his blood

Accept one another as Christ has accepted you

6) Read Romans 15:7. In this verse, Paul reminds the Christians at Rome that they have been *received* (that is, "accepted") by Christ. This theme is echoed in 1:6. What is so significant about this concept?

Because sin has put a barrier, but God has removed them

7) What aspect of our salvation mentioned in 2 Corinthians 5:21 makes us acceptable in God's sight?

God made him "sin" who had no to be sin for us, so that we might become the righteousness in him.

Summing Up . . .

"During the great depression of the 1930s, many banks would allow their customers to withdraw no more than 10 percent of their accounts during a given period of time because the banks did not have enough reserves to cover all deposits.

"But God's heavenly bank has no such limitations or restrictions. No Christian, therefore, has reason to be spiritually deprived, undernourished, or impoverished. In fact, he has no reason not to be completely healthy and immeasurably rich in the things of God. The Lord's heavenly resources are more than adequate to cover all our past debts, all our present liabilities, and all our future needs—and still not reduce the heavenly assets. That is the marvel of God's gracious provision for His children."—*John MacArthur*

Reflecting on the Text

8) In his classic book *All of Grace*, Charles Spurgeon tells a story of a minister who called on a poor woman with a desire to help her out of her financial straits. Money in hand, he knocked on her door repeatedly, but she did not answer. Eventually he left. Later, he related the incident to her at church. "Oh dear," she said, "I heard you, sir, and I'm so sorry I did not answer. I thought you were the man calling for the rent."

How does this story illustrate God's tremendous blessing of salvation and our tendency to misunderstand (and miss out on) the blessings that God offers us?

We think God is coming to demand payment from us, instead of come with full payment.

9) What one truth has impacted your life the most from this passage and why?

10) Have you been living as though the "good news" is not all that good? If so, what specific steps can you take this week to live out your great salvation?

_____

_____

_____

_____

Recording Your Thoughts

_____

_____

_____

_____

_____

_____

_____

_____

_____

_____

_____

_____

For further study, see the following passages:

Deuteronomy 7:6	Isaiah 45:4	Matthew 3:1–2
John 5:40	John 6:44	Romans 5:20
2 Corinthians 1:21	Philippians 2:13	Philippians 3:9
Colossians 1:13	2 Thessalonians 1:11–12	

Prayers That Please the Father

Opening Thought

1) Consider the following prayers:

"Lord, bless us today."

"Father, please help me find a parking spot close to the entrance."

"God, forgive me where I've failed you, and help me to live for you today."

What's right with these prayers? What (if anything) is wrong with them? Are they typical of most Christians you know? Or atypical?

The first one is so general - besides He always does bless us.

This looks suspiciously like using God for our own comfort & convenience, as if He were a celestial errand boy. However, I have prayed this prayer.

This one at least seems sincere, but it might be better to ask God to reveal where we are failing Him

Focus on self, not God

Take time - Create an atmosphere of thanksgiving

Background of the Passage

Twice in the first three chapters of Ephesians (see also 3:14–21), while discussing the marvelous acts of God for the elect and the great spiritual inheritance that believers in Christ possess, the Apostle Paul spontaneously erupts into prayers of thanksgiving and praise.

Remember, this was a church that was near and dear to the heart of the great apostle (see Acts 20:17–38). His affection for this particular flock and his passion to see them grasp the glorious riches of grace drove him to his knees.

With a backdrop of God's cosmic plan of salvation and in light of eternity, Paul's intercession takes on a weighty quality. He makes no trivial requests here. These recorded prayers serve as a wonderful model for how to pray for those we love and have been given responsibility to care for in the faith. Inspired as they are by the Holy Spirit, they also reveal the priorities that are on God's heart for his people.

Let's look now at the kind of prayer that pleases the Father.

Bible Passage

Read 1:15–23, noting the key words and definitions to the right of the passage.

Ephesians 1:15–23

15 *Therefore I also, after I heard of your* faith *in the Lord Jesus and your* love *for all the saints,*

16 *do not cease to give thanks for you, making mention of you in my prayers:*

17 *that the God of our Lord Jesus Christ, the Father of glory, may give to you the* spirit of wisdom and revelation *in the knowledge of Him,*

18 *the eyes of your understanding being enlightened; that you may know what is the hope of His calling, what are the riches of the glory of His inheritance in the saints,*

19 *and what [is] the exceeding greatness of His power toward us who believe, according to the working of His mighty power*

love for all the saints (v. 15)—the hallmark of God's people (1 John 4:8, 20–21)

do not cease (v. 16)—an echo of the same idea found in 1 Thessalonians 5:17

spirit of wisdom and revelation (v. 17)—a disposition of godly knowledge and insight that is possible only for a redeemed, sanctified mind

enlightened (v. 18)—illumined or given light, a reference to the Holy Spirit's ministry of continually illuminating spiritual truth for the child of God

20 which He worked in Christ when He raised Him from the dead and seated [Him] at His right hand in the heavenly [places],

21 far above all principality and power and might and dominion, and every name that is named, not only in this age but also in that which is to come.

22 And He put all [things] under His feet, and gave Him [to be] head over all [things] to the church,

23 which is His body, the fullness of Him who fills all in all.

exceeding greatness of His power (v. 19)—The same awesome power that raised Christ from the dead and exalted him into heaven is made available to every believer in Christ.

principality and power and might and dominion (v. 21)— terms used frequently in Jewish writings to designate the various ranks of angelic powers

Understanding the Text

2) What characteristic(s) of the Ephesians prompted Paul to be thankful? Why?

Your faith in the Lord Jesus
Your love for all the saints
These are evidences of Gods authentic work in their lives, and evidence that his ministry to them was "not in vain"

3) Paul prayed that the Ephesians' "spiritual eyes" might be opened and that they might come consequently into a deeper knowledge of God. Why was this foremost among the apostle's concerns for his flock?

Understanding is the key. Their faith would be sustained and their love increased by a deeper understanding of Gods character, what he has done for them, etc.
If we have these things, we are equipped

(verses to consider: Isaiah 6:1–8; John 17:3; Philippians 3:8–11)

Isaiah's vision of the holy God

15

4) How does Paul describe the power of God? What is significant about the fact that Paul prays for the Ephesians to "know" this power rather than to "receive" this power?

It is God's power, not ours. When He works through us, it is truly He who does it. We don't act independently from God. Implies experience

Cross-Reference

Read the following passage and consider how Paul and his associates prayed for the Colossian believers under their care.

Colossians 1:9–12

9 *For this reason we also, since the day we heard it, do not cease to pray for you, and to ask that you may be filled with the knowledge of His will in all wisdom and spiritual understanding;*

10 *that you may walk worthy of the Lord, fully pleasing [Him], being fruitful in every good work and increasing in the knowledge of God;*

11 *strengthened with all might, according to His glorious power, for all patience and longsuffering with joy;*

12 *giving thanks to the Father who has qualified us to be partakers of the inheritance of the saints in the light.*

Exploring the Meaning

5) In what ways does this passage specifically echo the Pauline teaching that right thinking leads to right living?

Knowledge of His will → that you may walk worthy

6) Colossians 3:2 says, "Set your mind on things above, not on things on the earth." How does this admonition relate to the manner in which Paul prayed?

Paul was always looking at the spiritual world, not counting the "mundane" as the most important thing

Didn't pray for "stuff" - comfort, but for deep realization of God's blessing - to VALUE

(verses to consider: Matthew 6:33; 2 Corinthians 4:18)

7) How should the truth that Christ is exalted above all (1:20–23) alter the way Christians live every day?

God's blessings are eternal, not passing away. "Spiritual" = love

If God truly rules

Eyes enlightened

Summing Up . . .

"God's deeper truths cannot be seen with our eyes, heard with our ears, or comprehended by our reason or intuition. They are revealed only to those who love Him."—*John MacArthur*

Reflecting on the Text

8) Someone has said, "The purpose of prayer is not to inform God of our needs, but to invite Him to rule our lives."

How does this statement compare with the sample prayers cited at the beginning of this lesson?

If you're inviting Him to rule

9) How would you assess your current prayer life? Is it honoring God? What needs to change about the content and frequency of your intercession?

I seldom pray — Against spiritual eyes. Need more understanding of dynamics of prayer. Intercession. Talking to God about everything

10) Write a prayer of thanks (or confession) to God in response to this lesson.

Recording Your Thoughts

_____

_____

_____

_____

_____

_____

_____

_____

_____

_____

_____

_____

_____

_____

_____

_____

_____

_____

For further study, see the following passages:

Psalm 8:6	John 13:34–35	Acts 1:8
Romans 1:5–6	Romans 8:29	1 Corinthians 12:12–27
Colossians 1:18	Colossians 1:29	Hebrews 2:8
1 John 3:2	1 John 4:16–18	Revelation 20:10–15

Additional Notes

Amazing Grace!

Opening Thought

1) Perhaps the most discussed and debated religious question on earth is:

How does a person make it to heaven?
or
How can someone know that he or she is right with God?

If you interviewed people on the street (using these questions), what varied responses would you get?

_____

_____

_____

_____

_____

_____

_____

_____

_____

_____

_____

_____

_____

Background of the Passage

On the question of eternal salvation, people generally take one of only two broad viewpoints. One very common cultural view says that *we* are individually responsible for our own destiny; that how well we live determines where we will spend eternity; that salvation is largely, if not entirely, dependent upon human effort.

This view is popular because it appeals to human pride. It makes us feel in control. It gives us the sense that we can earn our own way. Besides, the notion of having to ask for help is galling to successful people who fancy themselves as independent and who imagine that they are basically decent.

The other position says that salvation is a no-strings attached gift from God. We cannot possibly earn it, because we are sinful to the core. To paraphrase the words of C. S. Lewis, we are not basically nice people who need only to clean up our acts a bit, we are rebels who need to lay down our arms. Because of our sin, we are spiritually dead. Thus, it's only when we respond to God's gracious overtures, admit our sinfulness and helplessness, and humbly receive Christ's offer of forgiveness and eternal life that we find life.

Obviously, this latter view is unpopular. It is an affront to self-made men and women who want to live without acknowledging or relying upon the Creator. Yet, as we will see in this lesson, *this* view is taught in Scripture.

Bible Passage

Read 2:1–10, noting the key words and definitions to the right of the passage.

Ephesians 2:1–10

1 *And you [He made alive], who were dead in trespasses and sins,*

2 *in which you once walked according to the course of this world, according to the prince of the power of the air, the spirit who now works in the sons of disobedience,*

3 *among whom also we all once conducted ourselves in the lusts of our flesh, fulfilling the*

dead in trespasses and sins (v. 1)—total depravity and lostness resulting in an utter inability to know or please God

course of this world (v. 2)—a reference to the ungodly world structure, that system of entities and mind-sets that sets itself up against God and His rule

desires of the flesh and of the mind, and were by nature children of wrath, just as the others.

⁴ But God, who is rich in mercy, because of His great love with which He loved us,

⁵ even when we were dead in trespasses, made us alive together with Christ (by grace you have been saved),

⁶ and raised [us] up together, and made [us] sit together in the heavenly [places] in Christ Jesus,

⁷ that in the ages to come He might show the exceeding riches of His grace in [His] kindness toward us in Christ Jesus.

⁸ For by grace you have been saved through faith, and that not of yourselves; [it is] the gift of God,

⁹ not of works, lest anyone should boast.

¹⁰ For we are His workmanship, created in Christ Jesus for good works, which God prepared beforehand that we should walk in them.

children of wrath (v. 3)—the rebellious unregenerates who stand condemned before God

rich in mercy (v. 4)—God lavishes compassion and pity on those He loves, despite their abject sinfulness.

made us alive (v. 5)—a reference to the supernatural act of regeneration, but also with the added nuance of sustaining and preserving life

workmanship (v. 10)—can have the connotation of a work of art

Understanding the Text

2) How does Paul graphically describe those who are dead in sin? How does this compare to your experience?

_____

_____

_____

_____

_____

(verses to consider: 4:17–19; Romans 8:10)

3) What words does Paul use in the passage to describe God's actions toward the lost?

_____

_____

_____

_____

_____

> *Underline the word "grace" in this short passage.*

4) Verses 8 and 9 are the Bible's most concise statement of "salvation by grace through faith." This is the essence of the Christian gospel, and yet it has been the source of heated dispute.

To what does the word "that" in verse 8 refer? If we say that our faith is not also part of God's gracious gift to us, what then does that imply about the capabilities of spiritually dead people?

_____

_____

_____

_____

Cross-Reference

Romans 5:6–11

6 *For when we were still without strength, in due time Christ died for the ungodly.*

7 *For scarcely for a righteous man will one die; yet perhaps for a good man someone would even dare to die.*

8 *But God demonstrates His own love toward us, in that while we were still sinners, Christ died for us.*

9 *Much more then, having now been justified by His blood, we shall be saved from wrath through Him.*

10 *For if when we were enemies we were reconciled to God through the death of His Son, much more, having been reconciled, we shall be saved by His life.*

11 *And not only [that], but we also rejoice in God through our Lord Jesus Christ, through whom we have now received the reconciliation.*

Exploring the Meaning

5) What themes in this passage from Romans echo the message of 2:1–10?

_____

_____

_____

_____

_____

_____

6) What is significant about the truth that God saved us at our worst, "while we were still sinners," or, in the words of chapter 2, when we were "dead in trespasses"?

_____

_____

_____

_____

_____

_____

_____

7) How does John 6:44 contribute to your understanding of this passage?

_____

_____

_____

_____

_____

Summing Up . . .

"When we accept the finished work of Christ on our behalf, we act by the faith supplied by God's grace. . . . When a person chokes or drowns and stops breathing, there is nothing he can do. If he ever breathes again, it will be because someone else starts him breathing. A person who is spiritually dead cannot even make a decision of faith unless God first breathes into him the breath of spiritual life. Faith is simply breathing the breath that God's grace supplies. Yet, the paradox is that we must exercise it and bear the responsibility if we do not."—*John MacArthur*

Reflecting on the Text

8) In explaining this passage, Charles Spurgeon wrote this:

"Faith occupies the position of a channel or conduit pipe. Grace is the fountain and the stream. Faith is the aqueduct along which the mercy flood flows down to refresh the thirsty sons of men. . . . I remind you again that faith is only the channel or the aqueduct, and not the fountainhead. We must not look to it so much that we exalt it above the divine source of all blessing which lies in the grace of God."

Why is grace prior to and preeminent to faith?

_____

_____

_____

_____

_____

9) What new insights have you gained through this study into the marvelous grace of God?

_____

_____

_____

_____

_____

10) What can you do to "grow in the grace . . . of our Lord and Savior Jesus Christ" (2 Peter 3:18) this week?

_____

_____

_____

_____

_____

Recording Your Thoughts

_____

_____

_____

_____

_____

_____

_____

_____

_____

_____

For further study, see the following passages:

Matthew 12:35	John 1:9	John 15:8
Romans 3:20	Romans 6:1–7	Romans 8:29–30
2 Corinthians 10:4–5	Galatians 2:16	Titus 2:14
James 2:16–26	1 Peter 1:4	Revelation 7:10–12

Additional Notes

The Mystery of Unity in Christ

Ephesians 2:11—3:13

Opening Thought

"It is part of sinful human nature to build barriers that shut out other people."—*John MacArthur*

1) What examples of disunity and division, segregation and schism, have you observed within the last month?

_____

_____

_____

_____

_____

_____

_____

_____

_____

_____

_____

_____

_____

_____

Background of the Passage

Ever since the rebellion in Eden shattered the relationship between humans and God, plunging the human race into sin and judgment, people have found it impossible to co-exist peacefully. Consider that the very first child born on planet Earth, Cain, murdered his own brother, Abel, in an act of pre-meditated, jealous rage. This despicable act merely foreshadowed the enmity that would haunt the human race.

Every marriage, family, church (including, apparently, the church at Ephesus), community, and nation struggles every day to maintain harmony and peace. Humanity's fallenness creates powerful feelings of alienation and suspicion, leading to misunderstandings, disagreements, factions, conflict, and even outright war.

Though the barriers between people, spouses, neighbors, and nations often seem insurmountable, the Bible gives real hope and the only lasting answer for overcoming the grim prospect of hostility.

Christ is the Prince of Peace. He alone can bring us into right relationship with God. He alone can shatter the walls of antagonism and malice that separate human beings.

Consider the amazing truth found in the following passage.

Bible Passage

Read 2:11—3:13, noting the key words and definitions to the right of the passage.

Ephesians 2:11—3:13

11 *Therefore remember that you, once Gentiles in the flesh—who are called Uncircumcision by what is called the Circumcision made in the flesh by hands—*

12 *that at that time you were without Christ, being aliens from the commonwealth of Israel and strangers from the covenants of promise, having no hope and without God in the world.*

13 *But now in Christ Jesus you who once were far*

Gentiles (v. 11)—The Greek word is "ethnos," from which we get our English term "ethnic," it also signifies the non-Jewish world.

the middle wall of separation (v. 14)—an allusion to a wall in the Jewish temple that separated the court of the Gentiles from the areas accessible only to the Jews

off have been brought near by the blood of Christ.

¹⁴ For He Himself is our peace, who has made both one, and has broken down the middle wall of separation,

¹⁵ having abolished in His flesh the enmity, [that is], the law of commandments [contained] in ordinances, so as to create in Himself one new man [from] the two, [thus] making peace,

¹⁶ and that He might reconcile them both to God in one body through the cross, thereby putting to death the enmity.

¹⁷ And He came and preached peace to you who were afar off and to those who were near.

¹⁸ For through Him we both have access by one Spirit to the Father.

¹⁹ Now, therefore, you are no longer strangers and foreigners, but fellow citizens with the saints and members of the household of God,

²⁰ having been built on the foundation of the apostles and prophets, Jesus Christ Himself being the chief [cornerstone],

²¹ in whom the whole building, being joined together, grows into a holy temple in the Lord,

²² in whom you also are being built together for a dwelling place of God in the Spirit.

¹ For this reason I, Paul, the prisoner of Christ Jesus for you Gentiles—

² if indeed you have heard of the dispensation of the grace of God which was given to me for you,

³ how that by revelation He made known to me the mystery (as I have briefly written already,

⁴ by which, when you read, you may understand my knowledge in the mystery of Christ),

⁵ which in other ages was not made known to the sons of men, as it has now been revealed by the Spirit to His holy apostles and prophets:

⁶ that the Gentiles should be fellow heirs, of the same body, and partakers of His promise in Christ through the gospel,

one new man (v. 15)—The Greek word translated "new" refers to something utterly unlike anything before it. The idea is that all who come to Christ comprise a new entity in which all labels, except the label "Christian," are obsolete. The believer is different in kind and quality. Spiritually, a new person in Christ is neither Jew nor Gentile but Christian only.

reconcile (v. 16)—to change or exchange; to turn from hostility to friendship

putting to death the enmity (v. 16)—The death of Christ killed the hostility between a holy God and sinful people.

members of the household of God (v. 19)—God's family

a dwelling place of God in the Spirit (v. 22)—In contrast to Old Testament times when God's presence was temporarily localized in the Temple, now God takes up residence permanently in His Body, the Church.

partakers of his promise (v. 6)—The Gentiles share in the grace of God; this word was used in extra-biblical Greek to describe "joint possessors" of a house.

boldness and access (v. 12)—Faith in an all-sufficient Savior makes us acceptable to God and is the basis of our access into the presence of God.

tribulations (v. 13)—the frequent pressures and troubles that Paul encountered as he carried out his apostolic task (see 2 Corinthians 11:22–29)

⁷ *of which I became a minister according to the gift of the grace of God given to me by the effective working of His power.*

⁸ *To me, who am less than the least of all the saints, this grace was given, that I should preach among the Gentiles the unsearchable riches of Christ,*

⁹ *and to make all see what [is] the fellowship of the mystery, which from the beginning of the ages has been hidden in God who created all things through Jesus Christ;*

¹⁰ *to the intent that now the manifold wisdom of God might be made known by the church to the principalities and powers in the heavenly [places],*

¹¹ *according to the eternal purpose which He accomplished in Christ Jesus our Lord,*

¹² *in whom we have boldness and access with confidence through faith in Him.*

¹³ *Therefore I ask that you do not lose heart at my tribulations for you, which is your glory.*

Understanding the Text

2) How did Paul describe the spiritual plight of the Gentiles and in what ways did the Jews have an advantage?

_____

_____

_____

_____

(verses to consider: Romans 3:1–2; 9:4)

3) How would Paul's words have been initially received by both the Jewish and Gentile members of the Ephesian church?

_____

_____

_____

_____

4) In your own words, summarize the mystery revealed to Paul and set forth in this passage.

_____

_____

_____

Cross-Reference

Consider how the following passage from 2 Corinthians 5:16–21 relates to the message of 2:11—3:13.

16 *Therefore, from now on, we regard no one according to the flesh. Even though we have known Christ according to the flesh, yet now we know [Him thus] no longer.*

17 *Therefore, if anyone [is] in Christ, [he is] a new creation; old things have passed away; behold, all things have become new.*

18 *Now all things [are] of God, who has reconciled us to Himself through Jesus Christ, and has given us the ministry of reconciliation,*

19 *that is, that God was in Christ reconciling the world to Himself, not imputing their trespasses to them, and has committed to us the word of reconciliation.*

20 *Now then, we are ambassadors for Christ, as though God were pleading through us: we implore [you] on Christ's behalf, be reconciled to God.*

21 *For He made Him who knew no sin [to be] sin for us, that we might become the righteousness of God in Him.*

Exploring the Meaning

5) What does this passage add to the startling notion that in Christ, *everything* changes?

_____

_____

_____

_____

6) What is the practical significance of the truth expressed in 2 Corinthians 5:17 for relational conflict in marriages, families, churches, and between races and nations?

_____

_____

_____

_____

7) If Christ is the great reconciler, and we are his "ambassadors," what does this mean? What does an ambassador do?

_____

_____

_____

_____

Summing Up . . .

"During World War II a group of American soldiers was exchanging fire with some Germans who occupied a farm house. The family who lived in the house had run to the barn for protection. Suddenly their little three-year-old daughter became frightened and ran out into the field between the two groups of soldiers. When they saw the little girl, both sides immediately ceased firing until she was safe. A little child brought peace, brief as it was, as almost nothing else could have done.

"Jesus Christ came as a babe to earth, and in his sacrifice on the cross He Himself became peace for those who trust in Him. His peace was not temporary but permanent."—*John MacArthur*

Reflecting on the Text

8) In *The Cross of Peace*, Sir Philip Gibbs has written:
"The problem of fences has grown to be one of the most acute that the world must face. Today there are all sorts of zig-zag and criss-crossing fences running through the races and peoples of the world. Modern progress has made the world a neighborhood and God has given us the task of making it a brotherhood."

Is this just wishful thinking? How is this really possible?

_____

_____

_____

_____

_____

9) What act of reconciliation do you sense God leading you to pursue as a result of this study?

_____

_____

_____

_____

10) Make a list of wounded relationships for which you will pray for healing.

_____

_____

_____

_____

Recording Your Thoughts

_____
_____
_____
_____
_____
_____
_____
_____
_____
_____
_____
_____
_____
_____
_____
_____
_____
_____
_____

For further study, see the following passages:

Psalm 118:22	Isaiah 9:6	Isaiah 49:6
Isaiah 57:19	Acts 2:39	Acts 4:11
Acts 13:46–47	Romans 8:18	Romans 10:12–13
Galatians 3:28	Galatians 4:6–7	Colossians 1:19–23
Colossians 2:3	1 Timothy 1:12,13	Hebrews 4:15–16
1 Peter 2:5		

Power for the Church

Opening Thought

Imagine in your town a homeless person who is notorious for his unkempt appearance and desperate existence. He sleeps on heating grates and eats out of restaurant dumpsters. He spurns all offers of help.

Now imagine that this man dies, and authorities subsequently discover he was actually the heir to a vast fortune. In fact, the papers report that the penniless pauper died with more than a billion dollars in the bank!

1) What would you conclude about the man?

_____

_____

_____

_____

_____

_____

_____

_____

_____

_____

Background of the Passage

Many churchgoers are woefully ignorant of the vast spiritual wealth that is theirs in Christ. Others (even many true believers) know a good deal about the Bible and the Christian faith, and yet fail to live by these truths.

Either way, a meager spiritual existence is a tragedy, for as Paul reminded the Ephesians in the first part of his epistle, the children of God possess riches and resources beyond measure. We have the capacity to experience an abundant life (John 10:10).

In order for God to receive the glory He deserves and in order for us to find the fulfillment and purpose for which we were created, we need God to move in our hearts. We need illumination and motivation. It is important that we not only understand the truth of all that we possess in Christ, but also that we are divinely enabled to live out our great salvation.

This is Paul's magnificent intercession for the Ephesians. In a passionate pastoral prayer he gives a glimpse of the kind of rich existence that is possible when we are "filled with all the fullness of God."

Bible Passage

Read 3:14–21, noting the key words and definitions to the right of the passage.

Ephesians 3:14–21

14 *For this reason I bow my knees to the Father of our Lord Jesus Christ,*

15 *from whom the whole family in heaven and earth is named,*

16 *that He would grant you, according to the riches of His glory, to be strengthened with might through His Spirit in the inner man,*

17 *that Christ may dwell in your hearts through faith; that you, being rooted and grounded in love,*

18 *may be able to comprehend with all the saints*

Father (v. 14)—Our awesome Creator is simultaneously a tender, loving, concerned, compassionate divine Parent who welcomes and invites His children to come to Him.

according to the riches of His glory (v. 16)—The limitless riches of God's power are available for the spiritual welfare of every believer.

strengthened (v. 16)—fortified, braced, invigorated

what [is] the width and length and depth and height—

¹⁹ to know the love of Christ which passes knowledge; that you may be filled with all the fullness of God.

²⁰ Now to Him who is able to do exceedingly abundantly above all that we ask or think, according to the power that works in us,

²¹ to Him [be] glory in the church by Christ Jesus to all generations, forever and ever. Amen.

inner man (v. 16)—the real person as opposed to merely the outer physical appearance

dwell (v. 17)—to live in, to settle down in, to take up residence

be filled (v. 19)—The Greek word means to make full and speaks of total dominance of the self by God.

exceedingly abundantly (v. 20)—beyond all measure; the highest comparison imaginable

Understanding the Text

2) Why does Paul pray for the inner strength of the Spirit?

_____

_____

_____

_____

_____

3) What is the significance of the fact that Christ dwells in our hearts through faith?

_____

_____

_____

_____

_____

4) What does it mean to "know the love of Christ which passes knowledge"?

_____

_____

_____

_____

_____

_____

Cross-Reference

Consider this companion passage that sheds more light on the love of God.

Romans 8:31–39

31 *What then shall we say to these things? If God [is] for us, who [can be] against us?*

32 *He who did not spare His own Son, but delivered Him up for us all, how shall He not with Him also freely give us all things?*

33 *Who shall bring a charge against God's elect? [It is] God who justifies.*

34 *Who [is] he who condemns? [It is] Christ who died, and furthermore is also risen, who is even at the right hand of God, who also makes intercession for us.*

35 *Who shall separate us from the love of Christ? [Shall] tribulation, or distress, or persecution, or famine, or nakedness, or peril, or sword?*

36 *As it is written: "For Your sake we are killed all day long; We are accounted as sheep for the slaughter."*

37 *Yet in all these things we are more than conquerors through Him who loved us.*

38 *For I am persuaded that neither death nor life, nor angels nor principalities nor powers, nor things present nor things to come,*

39 *nor height nor depth, nor any other created thing, shall be able to separate us from the love of God which is in Christ Jesus our Lord.*

Exploring the Meaning

5) What in Paul's experience gave him such confidence in and assurance of the love of Christ?

_____

_____

_____

_____

_____

_____

6) What does John 14:23 say is required in order for Christ/God to be at home in the heart of a believer?

_____

_____

_____

_____

_____

_____

7) In what ways does Psalm 96 depict the fullness of God?

_____

_____

_____

_____

_____

_____

Summing Up . . .

"Spiritual power is not the mark of a special class of Christian, but is the mark of every Christian who submits to God's Word and Spirit. Like physical growth and strength, spiritual growth and strength do not come overnight. As we discipline our minds and spirits to study God's Word, understand it, and live by it, we are nourished and strengthened. Every bit of spiritual food and every bit of spiritual exercise add to our strength and endurance."

—John MacArthur

Reflecting on the Text

J. Wilbur Chapman often told of the testimony given by a certain man in one of his meetings:

"I got off at the Pennsylvania depot as a tramp, and for a year I begged on the streets for a living. One day I touched a man on the shoulder and said, 'Hey, mister, can you give me a dime?' As soon as I saw his face I was shocked to see that it was my own father. I said, 'Father, Father, do you know me?' Throwing his arms around me and with tears in his eyes, he said, 'Oh my son, at last I've found you! I've found you. You want a dime? Everything I have is yours.' Think of it. I was a tramp. I stood begging my own father for ten cents, when for eighteen years he had been looking for me to give me all that he had."

8) How does this story illustrate both the behavior of many Christians and the desire of our Heavenly Father?

_____

_____

_____

_____

_____

_____

_____

9) What truth is most meaningful to you as you contemplate Paul's prayer for the believers at Ephesus?

_____

_____

_____

_____

_____

10) What concrete and specific step can you take today to make Christ more "at home in your heart"?

_____

_____

_____

_____

_____

Recording Your Thoughts

_____

_____

_____

_____

_____

_____

For further study, see the following passages:

Ezra 9:5–6	Matthew 5:48	John 8:39–42
Acts 1:8	Romans 5:5	Romans 8:9
Romans 16:25	1 Corinthians 12:13	2 Corinthians 4:16
Colossians 1:9–11	1 John 3:10	

Additional Notes

God's Pattern for the Church

Opening Thought

1) Churches resort to all manner of strategies and plans in their attempts to attract visitors and win converts. On a scale of 1 to 10, with 1 being "utterly worldly" and 10 being "completely God-honoring," rate the following habits/practices:

- sending the staff to a church growth seminar *2*
- bringing in Christian celebrities to speak or sing *depends on the motivation*
- building a big, new, multi-million dollar state-of-the-art facility
- having the pastor shave his head if attendance reaches a certain number
- incorporating video clips from popular movies into sermons
- putting great emphasis on "seeker services"
- hiring church consultants

_____

_____

_____

_____

_____

_____

_____

_____

_____

_____

Background of the Passage

After three chapters of solid instruction in the foundational truths of God, Paul takes a dramatic turn, shifting his emphasis from doctrine to duty, from principles to practice, from beliefs to behavior. He has set forth all the blessings, honors, and privileges of being a child of God. Now he reminds believers of their consequent obligations and requirements as members of God's family.

First, Paul explains to his beloved congregation in Ephesus that they must live up to their new identity and calling in Christ. Next, he describes the characteristics of true believers and how believers who are committed to the glory of God will live together in unity.

This unity cannot occur unless each individual does his or her part. God has given each member of His Church one or more gifts for the building up of the Body.

Corporately and individually we are to grow up, and to be on our guard against erroneous ideas spread by deceitful teachers.

To see how you can do your part to make your church all that God wants it to be, read and study the passage that follows.

Bible Passage

Read 4:1–16, noting the key words and definitions to the right of the passage.

Ephesians 4:1–16

¹ I, therefore, the prisoner of the Lord, beseech you to walk worthy of the calling with which you were called,
² with all lowliness and gentleness, with longsuffering, bearing with one another in love,
³ endeavoring to keep the unity of the Spirit in the bond of peace.
⁴ [There is] one body and one Spirit, just as you were called in one hope of your calling;

therefore (v. 1)—the transitional word that indicates Paul's shift from discussing doctrine to discussing duty

beseech (v. 1)—to call to one's side, with the intention of needing help; this word connotes strong feeling or desire and suggests pleading or begging

lowliness (v. 2)—a Greek word unique to the New Testament that

5 *one Lord, one faith, one baptism;*

6 *one God and Father of all, who [is] above all, and through all, and in you all.*

7 *But to each one of us grace was given according to the measure of Christ's gift.*

8 *Therefore He says: "When He ascended on high, He led captivity captive, And gave gifts to men."*

9 *(Now this, "He ascended" —what does it mean but that He also first descended into the lower parts of the earth?*

10 *He who descended is also the One who ascended far above all the heavens, that He might fill all things.)*

11 *And He Himself gave some [to be] apostles, some prophets, some evangelists, and some pastors and teachers,*

12 *for the equipping of the saints for the work of ministry, for the edifying of the body of Christ,*

13 *till we all come to the unity of the faith and of the knowledge of the Son of God, to a perfect man, to the measure of the stature of the fullness of Christ;*

14 *that we should no longer be children, tossed to and fro and carried about with every wind of doctrine, by the trickery of men, in the cunning craftiness of deceitful plotting,*

15 *but, speaking the truth in love, may grow up in all things into Him who is the head—Christ—*

16 *from whom the whole body, joined and knit together by what every joint supplies, according to the effective working by which every part does its share, causes growth of the body for the edifying of itself in love.*

describes the humble spirit that should mark all believers

gentleness (v. 2)—literally "meekness," strength under control, a mild spirit

longsuffering (v. 2)—literally "long-tempered," that is, patience

unity of the Spirit (v. 3)—the Spirit-bestowed oneness of all true believers

baptism (v. 5)—probably a reference to water baptism, post salvation

equipping of the saints (v. 12)—the act of restoring, making fit or complete; in this context, leading Christians from sin to obedience

no longer be children (v. 14)—God's expectation that spiritually immature believers should grow up in their understanding and behavior

every wind of doctrine (v. 14)—a reference to the beguiling spiritual error promulgated by deceitful teachers who lurked in the shadows of the Ephesian church (and still hinder God's work around the world today)

Understanding the Text

2) Paul begins this section of his letter with an urgent plea for the Ephesians to "walk worthy of the calling" with which they had been called. What does he mean by this? Why does he start with this topic?

They need to set their sights high, to realize the tremendous work God has done to give them all the spiritual blessing they have. They need to function in the consciousness of this

Circle every character quality that Paul
indicates should mark the life of a believer.

3) How does Paul describe the unity that believers ought to share?

It is characterized by peace. Our unity is not conformity, but an acceptance of the variety of gifts. We have many important things in common.

Underline every reference to unity
that you see in this passage.

4) What obstacles impede the maturing of an individual Christian or a whole congregation?

Ignorance, lack of discernment, pride (not wanting to admit the need for change) competitiveness, selfishness, laziness – unwillingness to develop and use gifts to serve

48

Cross-Reference

Romans 12:4–18

⁴ For as we have many members in one body, but all the members do not have the same function,

⁵ so we, [being] many, are one body in Christ, and individually members of one another.

⁶ Having then gifts differing according to the grace that is given to us, [let us use them]: if prophecy, [let us prophesy] in proportion to our faith;

⁷ or ministry, [let us use it] in [our] ministering; he who teaches, in teaching;

⁸ he who exhorts, in exhortation; he who gives, with liberality; he who leads, with diligence; he who shows mercy, with cheerfulness.

⁹ [Let] love [be] without hypocrisy. Abhor what is evil. Cling to what is good.

¹⁰ [Be] kindly affectionate to one another with brotherly love, in honor giving preference to one another;

¹¹ not lagging in diligence, fervent in spirit, serving the Lord;

¹² rejoicing in hope, patient in tribulation, continuing steadfastly in prayer;

¹³ distributing to the needs of the saints, given to hospitality.

¹⁴ Bless those who persecute you; bless and do not curse.

¹⁵ Rejoice with those who rejoice, and weep with those who weep.

¹⁶ Be of the same mind toward one another. Do not set your mind on high things, but associate with the humble. Do not be wise in your own opinion.

¹⁷ Repay no one evil for evil. Have regard for good things in the sight of all men.

¹⁸ If it is possible, as much as depends on you, live peaceably with all men.

Exploring the Meaning

5) In what ways do Paul's words to the church at Rome echo his challenge to the church at Ephesus?

He emphasizes that the diversity in the body is so that all may be served

6) How can the existence of different spiritual gifts help bring about unity and growth in the body of Christ? How do they sometimes spark controversy, and what should this tell us?

_____

_____

_____

_____

7) Put brackets around the words and phrases that Paul uses to describe a church or individual that needs to mature spiritually.

What are the signs that a church is immature?

_____

_____

_____

_____

Summing Up . . .

"Even the most biblical and efficient of church organizations will not produce spiritual maturity without the leadership of God's gifted ministers who are continually in prayer and in His Word. Administration and structure has its place, but it is far from the heart of spiritual church growth. The great need of the church has always been spiritual maturity rather than organizational restructuring. All the books on leadership, organization, and management offer little help to the dynamics of the church of Jesus Christ.
"Even less does the church need entertaining. God's people can use their talents in ways that glorify the Lord and give testimony of His grace, but when testimony turns to vaudeville, as it often does, God is not glorified and His people are not edified. Religious entertainment neither comes from nor leads to spiritual maturity. It comes from self and can only promote self."

—*John MacArthur*

Reflecting on the Text

8) The skeptical German poet Heinrich Heine once said to some Christians: "You show me your redeemed life and I might be inclined to believe in your Redeemer."

How should this statement challenge the modern-day church?

_____

_____

_____

_____

9) What does God call His church to be and do in the midst of an evil age?

_____

_____

_____

_____

10) How does God possibly expect us to carry out all the difficult commands of Christ?

_____

_____

_____

_____

11) In what specific areas are you failing to "walk worthy of the calling with which you were called"?

_____

_____

_____

12) What practical steps will you take today to help your church grow into the local body God wants it to be?

_____

_____

_____

_____

Recording Your Thoughts

_____

_____

_____

_____

_____

_____

_____

_____

_____

_____

_____

For further study, see the following passages:

Deuteronomy 6:4	Psalm 68:18	Matthew 5:5
Acts 1:9–11	Romans 8:30	1 Corinthians 12:11–13
Philippians 1:21	Philippians 2:9–11	Colossians 2:19
1 Thessalonians 5:14, 21–22	2 Timothy 3:16–17	James 4:6
1 Peter 4:8		

Principles of New Life

Opening Thought

1) "Salvation is not a matter of improvement or perfection of what has previously existed. It is total transformation. The New Testament speaks of believers having a new mind, a new will, a new heart, a new inheritance, a new relationship, new power, new knowledge, new wisdom, new perception, new understanding, new righteousness, new love, new desire, new citizenship, and many other new things—all of which are summed up in newness of life (Romans 6:4).

"At the new birth a person becomes 'a new creature; the old things passed away; behold, new things have come' (2 Corinthians 5:17). It is not simply that he receives something new but that he *becomes* someone new. . . . The new nature is not added to the old nature but replaces it. The transformed person is a completely new 'I.'"—*John MacArthur*

If this is true, why do Christians still struggle so with sin? Why are there hypocrites in the church? Why do churches often feature such reprehensible behavior?

_____

_____

_____

_____

_____

_____

Background of the Passage

In chapters one through three of this epistle, Paul presented for the Ephesians a glorious reminder of their riches in Christ. He treated them to a theological banquet, rich with meaty doctrine.

Next, in chapter four, Paul helps them digest this weighty truth. He shows them how, practically speaking, they can both internalize and utilize all they have received.

Paul is adamant. As the Ephesians grasp what God has done for them and in them, they should begin living out in practice what is already true of them in principle. They should live transformed lives with a decided difference between their old lifestyles and their new lives in Christ. They should be set apart from those around them. They should stand out.

Furthermore, as a collective body their interpersonal relationships should be marked by shocking, unearthly attitudes and actions. In a world overrun with bitterness, hatred, deception, and immorality, Paul's readers should be marked by love, forgiveness, truthfulness, and purity.

This remarkable passage should challenge us to put the old things behind us, and it should whet our appetites to begin living out our new identities.

Bible Passage

Read 4:17–32, noting the key words and definitions to the right of the passage.

Ephesians 4:17–32

17 *This I say, therefore, and testify in the Lord, that you should no longer walk as the rest of the Gentiles walk, in the futility of their mind,*

18 *having their understanding darkened, being alienated from the life of God, because of the ignorance that is in them, because of the blindness of their heart;*

19 *who, being past feeling, have given themselves*

walk (v. 17)—to conduct oneself in daily living

being past feeling (v. 19)—a reference to the moral dullness or insensitivity that marks unbelievers as they ignore God and their consciences

over to lewdness, to work all uncleanness with greediness.

20 But you have not so learned Christ,

21 if indeed you have heard Him and have been taught by Him, as the truth is in Jesus:

22 that you put off, concerning your former conduct, the old man which grows corrupt according to the deceitful lusts,   *direction*

23 and be renewed in the spirit of your mind,

24 and that you put on the new man which was created according to God, in true righteousness and holiness.

25 Therefore, putting away lying, "[Let] each one [of you] speak truth with his neighbor," for we are members of one another.

26 "Be angry, and do not sin": do not let the sun go down on your wrath,

27 nor give place to the devil.

28 Let him who stole steal no longer, but rather let him labor, working with [his] hands what is good, that he may have something to give him who has need.

29 Let no corrupt word proceed out of your mouth, but what is good for necessary edification, that it may impart grace to the hearers.

30 And do not grieve the Holy Spirit of God, by whom you were sealed for the day of redemption.

31 Let all bitterness, wrath, anger, clamor, and evil speaking be put away from you, with all malice.

32 And be kind to one another, tenderhearted, forgiving one another, just as God in Christ forgave you.

put off (v. 22)—to strip away as in taking off old dirty clothes; a reference to once and for all repentance from sin at salvation

the old man (v. 22)—the worn out, useless, and unconverted sinful nature

be renewed (v. 23)—Used only here in the New Testament, this phrase expresses that at salvation, God redeems a person's mind and gives him or her a completely new spiritual and moral capability.

the new man (v. 24)—a new creation, not a renovation of what was, but an entirely new (in species or character) entity

corrupt (v. 29)—foul, putrid, rotten, worthless, disgusting

edification (v. 29)—the act of being helpful, constructive, or uplifting

grieve the Holy Spirit (v. 30)—We cause sorrow to the Holy Spirit of *truth* when we act in unholy ways and lie to one another.

Understanding the Text

2) Paul argues that it is unthinkable for a Christian to act like an unbeliever. Why? What points does he use to make his case?

_____

_____

_____

_____

_____

> *Circle the various phrases Paul uses to describe unregenerate people.*

3) What does Paul mean when he speaks of being "renewed in the spirit of your mind"?

Getting truth into your mind

_____

_____

_____

> *Underline each command found in this passage.*

4) What are the characteristics of "the new man"?

Truthful, not angry, generous, hard working edifying in your speech, tenderhearted, forgiving – standing up for God

56

Cross-Reference

Consider how the message of Colossians 3:1–17 dovetails with Paul's challenge to the Ephesian church.

1 *If then you were raised with Christ, seek those things which are above, where Christ is, sitting at the right hand of God.*
2 *Set your mind on things above, not on things on the earth.*
3 *For you died, and your life is hidden with Christ in God.*
4 *When Christ [who is] our life appears, then you also will appear with Him in glory.*
5 *Therefore put to death your members which are on the earth: fornication, uncleanness, passion, evil desire, and covetousness, which is idolatry.*
6 *Because of these things the wrath of God is coming upon the sons of disobedience,*
7 *in which you yourselves once walked when you lived in them.*
8 *But now you yourselves are to put off all these: anger, wrath, malice, blasphemy, filthy language out of your mouth.*
9 *Do not lie to one another, since you have put off the old man with his deeds,*
10 *and have put on the new [man] who is renewed in knowledge according to the image of Him who created him,*
11 *where there is neither Greek nor Jew, circumcised nor uncircumcised, barbarian, Scythian, slave [nor] free, but Christ [is] all and in all.*
12 *Therefore, as [the] elect of God, holy and beloved, put on tender mercies, kindness, humility, meekness, longsuffering;*
13 *bearing with one another, and forgiving one another, if anyone has a complaint against another; even as Christ forgave you, so you also [must do].*
14 *But above all these things put on love, which is the bond of perfection.*
15 *And let the peace of God rule in your hearts, to which also you were called in one body; and be thankful.*
16 *Let the word of Christ dwell in you richly in all wisdom, teaching and admonishing one another in psalms and hymns and spiritual songs, singing with grace in your hearts to the Lord.*
17 *And [whatever] you do in word or deed, [do] all in the name of the Lord Jesus, giving thanks to God the Father through Him.*

Exploring the Meaning

5) How do Colossians 3:2 and 10 add to your understanding of 4:23?

Set your mind
renewed

6) In practical, everyday terms, how does a Christian "put off" or "put away" wrong attitudes and habits? What does it mean to "put on love" (v. 14)?

7) What would the world say about a group of believers who were "doers" of this truth from God's Word?

Summing Up . . .

"Biblical terminology . . . does not say that a Christian has two different natures. He has but one nature, the new nature of Christ. The old self dies and the new self lives; they do not coexist. It is not a remaining old nature but the remaining garment of sinful flesh that causes Christians to sin. The Christian is a single new person, a totally new creation, not a spiritual schizophrenic. It is the filthy coat of remaining humanness in which the new creation dwells that continues to hinder and contaminate his living. The believer as a total person is transformed but not yet wholly perfect. He has residing sin but no longer reigning sin (Romans 6:14). He is no longer the old man corrupted but is now the new man created in righteousness and holiness, awaiting full salvation (Romans 13:11)."—*John MacArthur*

Reflecting on the Text

8) It has been said that the only reliable evidence of a person's being saved is not a past experience of receiving Christ but a present life that reflects Christ.

How accurately does your life reflect the holiness and goodness of God?

_____

_____

_____

_____

_____

9) What is the Spirit of God saying to you as a result of this study? Do you feel more comforted or convicted? Why?

_____

_____

_____

_____

_____

10) Write a prayer that conveys your heart's desire to live in a way that pleases Him.

_____

_____

_____

_____

_____

Recording Your Thoughts

_____

_____

_____

_____

_____

_____

_____

_____

_____

_____

_____

For further study, see the following passages:

Exodus 20:15	Matthew 18:21–35	Luke 14:13–14
John 8:44	Acts 2:38–40	Romans 1:21–28, 32
Romans 12:1–2	1 Corinthians 2:9–16	Galatians 2:20
James 3:6–8	1 John 2:6	1 John 5:20

Walking in Love and Light

Opening Thought

1) Imagine a man in your church who claims to be a Christian. His testimony sounds legitimate, and he has a long history of church involvement. It is common knowledge, however, that this man's life is permeated by a number of glaring, long-term sins.

A friend of yours insists that if this man were *truly* a follower of Christ, he would turn away from his sins. Another friend says that we all struggle with various sins and that this man's failings just happen to be among the list of highly visible sins that are frowned upon in Christian circles.

Can a person be a Christian and still sin long-term in grievous ways?

There is great reason for doubt. "I show you my faith by my works." It would be hard to know another person's motivations. God is the judge

Background on the Passage

The Ephesian congregation of believers lived in a pagan city. Not only were they surrounded by immorality, ungodliness, and decadence, but all of them had been saved from such a background.

After describing God's amazing salvation and the incomparable riches that all believers in Christ possess (chapters 1—3), Paul turns his attention to the practical ramifications of the gospel. He argues that if all these doctrines are true, and they *are*, then our lives will be different, in specific ways. Chapter four, then, begins to describe what life in Christ should look like.

The old ways are gone; we are "new men." God has gifted us and has called us to live together in a supernatural entity called the Church. In unity and love, we are to live to the glory of God.

While serving Him on earth, we are to become like Him. In the passage that follows, Paul describes how conformity to Christ contrasts to conformity with the world.

Bible Passage

Read 5:1–14, noting the key words and definitions to the right of the passage.

Ephesians 5:1–14

1 *Therefore be <u>imitators of God</u> as dear children.*
2 *And <u>walk in love</u>, as Christ also has loved us and <u>given Himself</u> for us, an offering and a sacrifice to God for a sweet-smelling aroma.*
3 *But fornication and all uncleanness or covetousness, let it not even be named among you, as is fitting for saints;*
4 *neither filthiness, nor foolish talking, nor coarse jesting, which are not fitting, but rather <u>giving of thanks</u>.*
5 *For this you know, that no fornicator, unclean person, nor covetous man, who is an idolater, has any inheritance in the kingdom of Christ and God.*

imitator (v. 1)—The Greek word from which comes the English word "mimic"; someone who copies specific characteristics of another person.

fornication (v. 3)—any kind of sexual sin or immorality.

foolish talking (v. 4)—A unique word in the New Testament made up of two Greek words: moros, from which comes moron = dull or stupid, and legos = to speak; intended to describe the conversation of someone intellectually deficient.

⁶ *Let no one deceive you with empty words, for because of these things the wrath of God comes upon the sons of disobedience.*

⁷ *Therefore do not be partakers with them.*

⁸ *For you were once darkness, but now [you are] light in the Lord. Walk as children of light*

⁹ *(for the fruit of the Spirit [is] in all goodness, righteousness, and truth),*

¹⁰ *finding out what is acceptable to the Lord.*

¹¹ *And have no fellowship with the unfruitful works of darkness, but rather expose [them].*

¹² *For it is shameful even to speak of those things which are done by them in secret.*

¹³ *But all things that are exposed are made manifest by the light, for whatever makes manifest is light.*

¹⁴ *Therefore He says: "Awake, you who sleep, Arise from the dead, And Christ will give you light."*

coarse jesting (v. 4)—sins of the tongue that include any speech that is obscene, degrading, suggestive, or immoral

has any inheritance (v. 5)—Those with life patterns of habitual immorality, impurity, or greed cannot inherit God's holy kingdom.

darkness (v. 8)—the character of the life of the unconverted as void of truth and virtue in intellectual and moral matters

have no fellowship (v. 11)—literally "do not become a partaker together with others"

expose (v. 11)—The believer's act of confronting and correcting evil in his own life and within the church.

it is shameful even to speak of those things (v. 12)—Some sins are so sordid that even describing them is morally and spiritually dangerous.

Understanding the Text

2) What does it mean to be an imitator of God? How is this possible? Who and what is our example?

_____

_____

_____

_____

_____

> Underline each reference to godly living.

3) How does Paul say the Christian's walk of love contrasts with the counterfeit ideas of love found in the world? *giving, not fearful*

Christian love - pure, action & truth from God. Motivated by Spirit, acknowledge Christ
World - words only, no reality no knowledge or experience of God.

(verses to consider: 1 John 3:18; 4:7–19)

4) What is the significance of the "light and darkness" metaphor used by Paul?

Tremendous contrast - opposites, cannot coexist when you're in darkness, the only solution is light
No light = no life

Cross-Reference

Galatians 5:16–26

16 *I say then: Walk in the Spirit, and you shall not fulfill the lust of the flesh.*
17 *For the flesh lusts against the Spirit, and the Spirit against the flesh; and these are contrary to one another, so that you do not do the things that you wish.*
18 *But if you are led by the Spirit, you are not under the law.*
19 *Now the works of the flesh are evident, which are: adultery, fornication, uncleanness, lewdness,*
20 *idolatry, sorcery, hatred, contentions, jealousies, outbursts of wrath, selfish ambitions, dissensions, heresies,*
21 *envy, murders, drunkenness, revelries, and the like; of which I tell you beforehand, just as I also told [you] in time past, that those who practice such things will not inherit the kingdom of God.*
22 *But the fruit of the Spirit is love, joy, peace, longsuffering, kindness, goodness, faithfulness,*

²³ *gentleness, self-control. Against such there is no law.*
²⁴ *And those [who are] Christ's have crucified the flesh with its passions and desires.*
²⁵ *If we live in the Spirit, let us also walk in the Spirit.*
²⁶ *Let us not become conceited, provoking one another, envying one another.*

Exploring the Meaning

5) How does this passage from Paul's Epistle to the Galatians enhance your understanding of 5:1–14?

_____

_____

_____

_____

_____

6) Paul lists here only two options for living: walking in the Spirit or fulfilling the lust of the flesh. What are the implications of this for lukewarm Christians who are not willing to fully submit to the Lordship of Christ? Are they truly Christians?

_____

_____

_____

_____

7) What insights do these passages from Paul give to believers who are charged with "being *in* the world, but not *of* the world"?

_____

_____

_____

_____

Summing Up . . .

"It is natural for children to be like their parents. They have their parents' nature, and they instinctively imitate their parents' actions and behavior. Through Jesus Christ, God has given us the right to become His children (John 1:12; Galatians 3:26). As Paul declared at the beginning of this letter, God 'predestined us to adoption as sons through Jesus Christ to Himself, according to the kind intention of His will' (1:5). Because our heavenly Father is holy, we are to be holy. Because He is kind, we are to be kind. Because He is forgiving, we are to be forgiving. Because God in Christ humbled himself, we are to humble ourselves. Because God is love, as His beloved children we are to walk in love. This ability is not natural, however, but supernatural—requiring a new nature and the continuous power of the Holy Spirit flowing through us by obedience to God's Word."—*John MacArthur*

Reflecting on the Text

8) History records that Alexander the Great once discovered a coward in his army, a soldier who happened to be named Alexander. The legendary leader confronted the man and thundered, "Renounce your cowardice or renounce your name!"

The implication for us is clear. We who bear the name "Christian" *must* reflect the character of Jesus Christ.

Do you? As you reflect on 5:1–14, what commands do you see that you are not obeying? What listed sins are you carelessly committing?

_____

_____

_____

_____

9) Do you tolerate evil and look the other way, or do you confront it gently and in love when you see it in your church or world?

_____

_____

_____

_____

10) Write a prayer to God summarizing your own personal application of this passage to your life (that is, how you'd like to be a "doer" of this truth):

_____

_____

_____

_____

Recording Your Thoughts

_____

_____

_____

_____

_____

_____

_____

_____

For further study, see the following passages:

Proverbs 4:18	Isaiah 60:1	Matthew 5:48
John 8:12	Romans 5:8–10	Romans 8:29
Romans 12:1–2	1 Corinthians 6:9–10	2 Corinthians 3:18
Colossians 1:13	Colossians 3:8	2 Thessalonians 3:6, 14
1 Peter 1:14–16	1 John 1:5–7	1 John 3:9–10

Additional Notes

Wise Living

Opening Thought

1) Death

Only a truly morbid individual constantly obsesses over his own eventual demise. On the other hand, only a foolish person refuses to ponder his own mortality.

It's true that we're not ready to live, until we're first ready to die.

What about you? Do you ever consider that God has granted you a fixed amount of time in this world and that every tick of the clock brings you that much closer to your date with eternity?

Ask yourself this sober question, "How well are you living this precious gift of life?"

Imagine you were to discover that you have one week to live. What regrets would you have? What unfinished business would fill you with sadness? Would you feel you have lived wisely, in a way that honors God? Why or why not?

_____

_____

_____

_____

_____

_____

Background on the Passage

The Apostle Paul wrote to a group of converts immersed in an evil culture. The Ephesian believers, much as we are, were surrounded by pagans who lived for the moment, who rejected the general revelation of God in creation and the special revelation of God in the gospel of Jesus Christ. This whole society focused on the worldly and trivial and indulged their every fleshly whim and desire.

This epitomizes foolishness: to ignore the reality of God, to reject His Lordship over one's life, to spurn His gracious offer of forgiveness, to live as though this world were all that is or ever will be.

Lest these old patterns of thinking creep back into the hearts and minds of the Ephesian believers, Paul urgently warns his brothers and sisters in the faith to remember the brevity of this life, the evil, deceptive nature of satanic counterfeits, and the wonderful prospect of walking in and living by the Spirit of God.

Only this kind of wise living, befitting our high calling in Christ, can bring joy now and reward in the life to come.

Bible Passage

Read 5:15–21, noting the key words and definitions to the right of the passage.

Ephesians 5:15–21

15 *See then that you walk circumspectly, not as fools but as wise,*
16 *redeeming the time, because the days are evil.*
17 *Therefore do not be unwise, but understand what the will of the Lord [is].*
18 *And do not be drunk with wine, in which is dissipation; but be filled with the Spirit,*
19 *speaking to one another in psalms and hymns and spiritual songs, singing and making melody in your heart to the Lord,*
20 *giving thanks always for all things to God the*

circumspectly (v. 15)—carefully, accurately, exactly; carries the idea of looking, examining, and investigating something with great intensity

redeeming (v. 16)—buying back; we are to buy all the time we have and devote it to the Lord

time (v. 16)—not seconds, minutes, and hours, but a fixed, measured, allocated season; that is, our individual lifetimes as believers

Father in the name of our Lord Jesus Christ,
21 *submitting to one another in the fear of God.*

do not be drunk with wine
(v. 18)—a reference to the drunken orgies commonly associated with pagan worship ceremonies in Ephesus

dissipation (v. 18)—excess; that is, a dissolute, debauched, profligate way of living

be filled with the Spirit
(v. 18)—to be under the influence of God's Spirit; to be dominated and controlled by the presence of Christ through His Word

psalms (v. 19)—Old Testament psalms put to music

hymns (v. 19)—Songs of praise, different from Old Testament psalms in that these likely praised the Lord Jesus Christ by name.

spiritual songs (v. 19)— probably songs of testimony

giving thanks always (v. 20)— Showing appreciation for who God is and gratitude for what He has done should mark the children of God.

submitting (v. 21)—humbling oneself before others—a characteristic of Spirit-filled believers.

Understanding the Text

2) Why was Paul so concerned that the Ephesians live wisely?

_____

_____

_____

_____

3) According to Paul, what are the evidences that a person is filled with the Spirit?

_____

_____

_____

_____

_____

(verses to consider: Acts 2:4; 4:8, 31; 6:3; Romans 8:9; 1 Corinthians 12:13)

4) Paul suggests that wisdom should lead believers to understand and do God's will. How can we know the will of God for our lives?

_____

_____

_____

_____

_____

Cross-Reference

Consider what King Solomon had to say about foolishness vs. wise living.

Proverbs 1:20–33

20 *Wisdom calls aloud outside; She raises her voice in the open squares.*

21 *She cries out in the chief concourses, At the openings of the gates in the city She speaks her words:*

22 *"How long, you simple ones, will you love simplicity? For scorners delight in their scorning, And fools hate knowledge.*

23 *Turn at my rebuke; Surely I will pour out my spirit on you; I will make my words known to you.*

24 *Because I have called and you refused, I have stretched out my hand and no one regarded,*

25 *Because you disdained all my counsel, And would have none of my rebuke,*

²⁶ *I also will laugh at your calamity; I will mock when your terror comes,*

²⁷ *When your terror comes like a storm, And your destruction comes like a whirlwind, When distress and anguish come upon you.*

²⁸ *"Then they will call on me, but I will not answer; They will seek me diligently, but they will not find me.*

²⁹ *Because they hated knowledge And did not choose the fear of the* LORD,

³⁰ *They would have none of my counsel [And] despised my every rebuke.*

³¹ *Therefore they shall eat the fruit of their own way, And be filled to the full with their own fancies.*

³² *For the turning away of the simple will slay them, And the complacency of fools will destroy them;*

³³ *But whoever listens to me will dwell safely, And will be secure, without fear of evil."*

Exploring the Meaning

5) In this passage, Solomon personifies wisdom. How does he describe her? How do the foolish react to her?

_____

_____

_____

_____

_____

Underline each word or phrase that describes the foolish.

6) What does this passage say will happen to those who submit to wisdom and conduct their lives according to her commands?

_____

_____

_____

_____

7) Is it possible to live a Spirit-filled existence apart from the Word of God (1:23). How do you know?

_____

_____

_____

_____

_____

Summing Up . . .

"To be filled with the Spirit involves confession of sin, surrender of will, intellect, body, time, talent, possessions, and desires. It requires the death of selfishness and the slaying of self-will. When we die to self, the Lord fills us with His Holy Spirit. . . .

"The filling of the Spirit is not an esoteric, mystical experience bestowed on the spiritual elite through some secret formula or other such means. It is simply taking the Word of Christ (Scripture) and letting it indwell and infuse every part of our being. To be filled with God's Spirit is to be filled with His Word. And as we are filled with God's Word, it controls our thinking and action, and we thereby come more and more under the Spirit's control."

—*John MacArthur*

Reflecting on the Text

8) Napoleon said: "There is in the midst of every great battle a ten to fifteen minute period that is the crucial point. Take that period and you win the battle; lose it and you will be defeated."

Bringing this principle over into the spiritual realm, what are some specific ways you need to be vigilant and careful today as you seek to walk with the Lord and serve Him?

_____

_____

_____

_____

_____

9) Are you making the most of the time God has given you? In light of the truth that your days are numbered, what trivial activities do you need to excise from your life and daily schedule?

_____

_____

_____

_____

_____

10) Carefully re-read today's passages. Review the quote that describes what it means to live by the Spirit. What should you do to live this kind of Spirit-filled life today?

_____

_____

_____

_____

_____

Recording Your Thoughts

_____

_____

_____

_____

_____

_____
_____
_____
_____
_____
_____
_____
_____

For further study, see the following passages:

2 Chronicles 5:12, 14	Psalm 33:1	Psalm 149:1
Proverbs 9:10	Proverbs 23:20–21, 29–35	Luke 4:1
Acts 16:25	Galatians 3:28	Galatians 5:16–23
Colossians 2:7	1 Thessalonians 4:3	1 Thessalonians 5:18
1 Timothy 2:3–4	1 Peter 2:13–15, 20	

Additional Notes

_____
_____
_____
_____
_____
_____
_____
_____
_____

God-honoring Relationships

Ephesians 5:22—6:9

Opening Thought

1) Rank the following descriptions 1–10 (with 1 being the *most* reliable indicator of a person who is pleasing to God and 10 being the *least* reliable indicator of spiritual maturity):

_____ Has entire New Testament memorized

_____ Has entire New Testament memorized *in Greek*

_____ Has one-hour daily quiet time

_____ Has two-hour daily quiet time

_____ Serves on church missions committee and goes on annual short term mission trips

_____ Teaches a popular Sunday school class on biblical theology

_____ Graduated from seminary with highest honors

_____ Seldom misses a church function or meeting

_____ Has a strong marriage and lots of healthy relationships

_____ Listens to Christian radio around-the-clock

What is the mark of true spiritual maturity? In other words, what kind of external behaviors/human activities are most pleasing to God?

_____

_____

_____

_____

_____

_____

_____

Background of the Passage

Paul's letter to the Ephesians began with three chapters of critical New Testament theology, emphasizing the believer's wealth in Christ. But Christianity is not a collection of abstract doctrines, an ivory tower religion of the mind. Paul contends in chapters 4—6 that true spirituality always reveals itself in the rough and tumble of everyday life.

Jesus simplified God's law to two commands to love—to love God and to love others (Matthew 22:25–29). This is the true measure of our faith. How fully do we love God? Is He uppermost in our affections?

Not only that, but how well do we care for our spouses, children, and neighbors? How well do we get along with our co-workers? If our faith doesn't show itself vividly in our interactions with other people, the onlooking world has every right to question the validity of our confession (John 13:34–35).

With the imperative to love in mind, chapters 5 and 6 address how we should act in our various relationships.

Bible Passage

Read 5:22—6:9, noting the key words and definitions to the right of the passage.

Ephesians 5:22—6:9

²² *Wives, submit to your own husbands, as to the Lord.*
²³ *For the husband is head of the wife, as also Christ is head of the church; and He is the Savior of the body.*
²⁴ *Therefore, just as the church is subject to Christ, so [let] the wives [be] to their own husbands in everything.*
²⁵ *Husbands, love your wives, just as Christ also loved the church and gave Himself for her,*
²⁶ *that He might sanctify and cleanse her with the washing of water by the word,*

submit (v. 22)—To voluntarily surrender one's rights, not out of subservience or servility but out of willingness to function under the other's leadership.

head (v. 23)—This word speaks of God-ordained authority and leadership.

love your wives just as Christ also loved the church (v. 25)—unreserved, selfless, sacrificial, unconditional love

27 that He might present her to Himself a glorious church, not having spot or wrinkle or any such thing, but that she should be holy and without blemish.

28 So husbands ought to love their own wives as their own bodies; he who loves his wife loves himself.

29 For no one ever hated his own flesh, but nourishes and cherishes it, just as the Lord [does] the church.

30 For we are members of His body, of His flesh and of His bones.

31 "For this reason a man shall leave his father and mother and be joined to his wife, and the two shall become one flesh."

32 This is a great mystery, but I speak concerning Christ and the church.

33 Nevertheless let each one of you in particular so love his own wife as himself, and let the wife [see] that she respects [her] husband.

1 Children, obey your parents in the Lord, for this is right.

2 "Honor your father and mother," which is the first commandment with promise:

3 "that it may be well with you and you may live long on the earth."

4 And you, fathers, do not provoke your children to wrath, but bring them up in the training and admonition of the Lord.

5 Bondservants, be obedient to those who are your masters according to the flesh, with fear and trembling, in sincerity of heart, as to Christ;

6 not with eyeservice, as men-pleasers, but as bondservants of Christ, doing the will of God from the heart,

7 with goodwill doing service, as to the Lord, and not to men,

8 knowing that whatever good anyone does, he will receive the same from the Lord, whether [he is] a slave or free.

sanctify...cleanse...holy...with out blemish (vv. 26–27)—The husband has a divine obligation to help lead his wife in purity to conformity with the image of Christ.

nourishes and cherishes (v. 29)—warm and tender affection, attentiveness, and care for needs

be joined to his wife (v. 31)—literally to be glued or cemented together

obey (v. 1)—literally "to hear under"; that is, to listen with attentiveness and with the intent to respond positively to what has been said

honor (vv. 2, 3)—to value highly, hold in the highest regard

do not provoke your children to wrath (v. 4)—Do not rule with domineering and authoritarian practices that crush the spirit of a child and cause him or her to lose heart.

fear and trembling (v. 5)—not actual fright but deep respect for authority

eyeservice, as men-pleasers (v. 6)—conscientious labor performed only in the boss' sight, but laziness when his back is turned

⁹ *And you, masters, do the same things to them, giving up threatening, knowing that your own Master also is in heaven, and there is no partiality with Him.*

giving up threatening (v. 9)— to loosen up, not throw one's weight around in an abusive or inconsiderate manner

Understanding the Text

2) What statements in 5:22–24 spark controversy? How does a careful reading of this entire section (vv. 22–31) refute most, if not all, of what the modern feminist movement claims about Christianity's view of women?

_____

_____

_____

_____

_____

3) What is the God-given role of a Christian wife?

_____

_____

_____

_____

_____

4) What is the God-given role of a Christian husband?

_____

_____

_____

_____

_____

Cross-Reference

Colossians 3:18—4:1

¹⁸ *Wives, submit to your own husbands, as is fitting in the Lord.*

¹⁹ *Husbands, love your wives and do not be bitter toward them.*

²⁰ *Children, obey your parents in all things, for this is well pleasing to the Lord.*

²¹ *Fathers, do not provoke your children, lest they become discouraged.*

²² *Bondservants, obey in all things your masters according to the flesh, not with eyeservice, as men-pleasers, but in sincerity of heart, fearing God.*

²³ *And whatever you do, do it heartily, as to the Lord and not to men,*

²⁴ *knowing that from the Lord you will receive the reward of the inheritance; for you serve the Lord Christ.*

²⁵ *But he who does wrong will be repaid for what he has done, and there is no partiality.*

¹ *Masters, give your bondservants what is just and fair, knowing that you also have a Master in heaven.*

Exploring the Meaning

5) Why do you suppose the parenting counsel in both of these passages was directed only to the fathers and not also to the mothers?

_____

_____

_____

_____

_____

_____

6) What are some of the primary ways parents "provoke" and "discourage" their children?

_____

_____

_____

_____

_____

_____

7) In the first century, Paul saw many abuses in slave/master relationships. What principles from the twin passages in Ephesians and Colossians can we draw for modern-day working relationships?

_____

_____

_____

_____

_____

_____

Summing Up . . .

"There are no classifications of Christians. Every believer in Jesus Christ has exactly the same salvation, the same standing before God, the same divine nature and resources, and the same divine promises and inheritance (Acts 10:34; Romans 2:11; James 1:1–9).

"But in matters of role and function God has made distinctions. Although there are no differences in intrinsic worth or basic spiritual privilege and rights among His people, the Lord has given rulers in government certain authority over the people they rule, to church leaders He has given authority over the church, to husbands He has delegated authority over their wives, to parents He has given authority over their children, and to employers He has given authority over employees."—*John MacArthur*

Reflecting on the Text

8) Growing within our culture is a widespread rebellion against authority. This distrust for those in positions of leadership is captured on the ubiquitous bumper sticker that reads "Question Authority."

Why is authority wise and good? What would the world be like if all authority vanished?

_____

_____

_____

_____

_____

9) Given what you've studied about God's intention for husbands, wives, children, and parents, what encourages you? What convicts you?

_____

_____

_____

_____

10) Specifically and practically, what can you do to be a better employee/employer this week?

_____

_____

_____

_____

_____

Recording Your Thoughts

_____

_____

_____

_____

_____

_____

_____

_____

_____

_____

_____

_____

_____

_____

_____

_____

_____

_____

_____

For further study, see the following passages:

Genesis 2:24	Exodus 20:12	Exodus 21:16, 26–27
Deuteronomy 5:16	Deuteronomy 23:15–16	Proverbs 13:24
Proverbs 17:21	Acts 10:34	Romans 2:11
1 Corinthians 11:3	2 Corinthians 11:23	Philippians 2:1–4
Titus 2:4–5	Hebrews 12:5–11	James 2:9
1 Peter 2:18		

Spiritual Warfare

Opening Thought

1) How has the American experience of war gradually changed throughout this century (from World Wars I and II, to Korea, to Vietnam, to the Gulf War, to the Kosovo conflict)? How has this altered the way modern generations perceive war?

_____

_____

_____

_____

_____

_____

_____

_____

_____

_____

_____

_____

_____

_____

_____

Background of the Passage

Paul's description of the true Christian, described in chapters 1—3, and the faithful Christian life, 4:1—6:9, lead him to an exposition on spiritual warfare in 6:10–20. The faithful Christian life is a battle—warfare on a grand scale—because when God begins to bless, Satan begins to attack.

If we are walking worthy of our calling, in humility rather than pride, in unity rather than divisiveness, in the new self rather than the old, in love rather than lust, in light rather than darkness, in wisdom rather than foolishness, in the fullness of the Spirit rather than the drunkenness of wine, and in mutual submission rather than self-serving independence, then we can be absolutely certain that we will have opposition and conflict.

The good news is that God does not leave His children unprepared or unprotected in this cosmic conflict. This passage is a heartening reminder of all that God has done and all that we must do to win the victory.

In Christ, not only can we withstand the devil's assaults, but we can also defeat the diabolical forces that are arrayed against God and His Church. The gates of hell cannot stand against us!

Bible Passage

Read 6:10–17, noting the key words and definitions to the right of the passage.

Ephesians 6:10–17

10 *Finally, my brethren, be strong in the Lord and in the power of His might.*

11 *Put on the whole armor of God, that you may be able to stand against the wiles of the devil.*

12 *For we do not wrestle against flesh and blood, but against principalities, against powers, against the rulers of the darkness of this age, against spiritual [hosts] of wickedness in the heavenly [places].*

13 *Therefore take up the whole armor of God, that*

be strong in the Lord and in the power of His might (v. 10)—Believers must rely completely on God's omnipotence to win the battle.

stand (v. 11)—to stand firm, in a military sense; to maintain a critical position while under attack

wiles (v. 11)—schemes; the Greek word from which comes the English term "methods." Carries the idea of craftiness, cunning, deception.

you may be able to withstand in the evil day, and having done all, to stand.

14 Stand therefore, having girded your waist with truth, having put on the breastplate of righteousness,

15 and having shod your feet with the preparation of the gospel of peace;

16 above all, taking the shield of faith with which you will be able to quench all the fiery darts of the wicked one.

17 And take the helmet of salvation, and the sword of the Spirit, which is the word of God;

wrestle (v. 12)—hand-to-hand combat

principalities . . . powers . . . rulers . . . spiritual [hosts] of wickedness (v. 12)—A description of the different strata and rankings of invisible, supernatural demons and evil spirits who are part of the devil's empire.

shod your feet (v. 15)—Roman soldiers wore boots with nails (cleats) in them to help brace their feet in all terrains. For the Christian, the gospel of peace with God gives sure footing and a sound foundation.

shield of faith (v. 16)—The word is the Greek term for the large 2.5 X 4.5 foot shields carried by soldiers to protect their entire bodies. As long as Christians place their trust in God, they will be protected.

fiery darts of the wicked one (v. 16)—In ancient times, arrows were often tipped with cloth, covered with pitch and ignited; the idea is that our faith affords us protection against the many temptations of the devil.

the helmet of salvation (v. 17)—protects the head, for Satan attacks a believer's assurance of salvation with his weapons of doubt and discouragement

the sword of the Spirit (v. 17)—The truth of Scripture, the only weapon that a Christian should carry into battle.

Understanding the Text

2) What does Paul mean when he states categorically that our fight is "not against flesh and blood"?

_____

_____

_____

_____

_____

> *Underline each word and phrase that describes our enemy and his/its activity.*

3) What protective (defensive) pieces of armor are children of God given in their ongoing struggle with the forces of evil? What weapons are we given with which to wage war?

_____

_____

_____

_____

_____

4) Why does Paul so emphasize the concept of *standing* (vv. 11, 13–14)?

_____

_____

_____

_____

_____

Cross-Reference

Consider the example of Christ in the famous account of His temptation by the devil. Note carefully how He waged spiritual warfare.

Luke 4:1–13

¹ Then Jesus, being filled with the Holy Spirit, returned from the Jordan and was led by the Spirit into the wilderness,

² being tempted for forty days by the devil. And in those days He ate nothing, and afterward, when they had ended, He was hungry.

³ And the devil said to Him, "If You are the Son of God, command this stone to become bread."

⁴ But Jesus answered him, saying, "It is written, 'Man shall not live by bread alone, but by every word of God.'"

⁵ Then the devil, taking Him up on a high mountain, showed Him all the kingdoms of the world in a moment of time.

⁶ And the devil said to Him, "All this authority I will give You, and their glory; for [this] has been delivered to me, and I give it to whomever I wish.

⁷ "Therefore, if You will worship before me, all will be Yours."

⁸ And Jesus answered and said to him, "Get behind Me, Satan! For it is written, 'You shall worship the LORD your God, and Him only you shall serve.'"

⁹ Then he brought Him to Jerusalem, set Him on the pinnacle of the temple, and said to Him, "If You are the Son of God, throw Yourself down from here.

¹⁰ "For it is written: 'He shall give His angels charge over you, To keep you,'

¹¹ "and, 'in their hands they shall bear you up, Lest you dash your foot against a stone.'"

¹² And Jesus answered and said to him, "It has been said, 'You shall not tempt the LORD your God.'"

¹³ Now when the devil had ended every temptation, he departed from Him until an opportune time.

Exploring the Meaning

5) What was Jesus' method for defending against the attack of Satan?

_____

_____

_____

_____

(verses to consider: Matthew 4:1–11; Luke 22:44)

6) Read 2 Corinthians 10:3–5. What extra insights into spiritual battle do you find in this passage? What is the tone of this passage? Why?

_____

_____

_____

_____

7) Read 1 Thessalonians 5:6–8. What should be the Christian's frame of mind?

_____

_____

_____

_____

_____

Summing Up . . .

"It is easy for believers—especially in the Western world, where the church is generally prosperous and respected—to be complacent and become oblivious to the seriousness of the battle around them. They rejoice in 'victories' that involve no battles and in a kind of peace that is merely the absence of conflict. Theirs is the victory and peace of the draft dodger or defector who refuses to fight. They are not interested in armor because they are not engaged in war.

"God gives no deferments or exemptions. His people are at war and will continue to be at war until He returns and takes charge of earth. But even the most willing and eager soldier of Christ is helpless without God's provision."—*John MacArthur*

Reflecting on the Text

8) "A Christian who no longer has to struggle against the world, the flesh and the devil is a Christian who has fallen into sin or into complacency. A Christian who has no conflict is a Christian who has retreated from the front lines of service."—*John MacArthur*

What does this study teach or remind you about spiritual warfare? How actively are you engaged in the cosmic conflict between God and His enemies?

_____

_____

_____

_____

_____

9) In what specific ways does Satan most often wage war against you? Why? How successfully are you resisting him?

_____

_____

_____

_____

10) Personalize this passage by turning it into a prayer and asking God to give you the grace to stand in His strength and to fight as you should.

_____

_____

_____

_____

Recording Your Thoughts

_____
_____
_____
_____
_____
_____
_____
_____
_____
_____
_____
_____
_____
_____
_____
_____
_____
_____
_____
_____

For further study, see the following passages:

Psalm 18:30　　　　　Proverbs 30:5–6　　　　Isaiah 59:17
2 Corinthians 4:4　　Philippians 4:13　　　　Colossians 2:15
2 Timothy 2:1　　　　Hebrews 4:12　　　　　1 Peter 3:22
1 Peter 5:8–9　　　　1 John 5:4

A Praying Church

Opening Thought

1) Imagine that you are granted the opportunity to "build the perfect church." From the following list you are allowed to pick only five components. Which of the following would you select? (Put a check mark beside your choices.)

_____ a brand-new, state-of-the-art multi-million dollar facility (debt-free)

_____ a gifted, talented, unified staff

_____ an operating budget of $1 million per month

_____ a congregation enthusiastic about and trained for evangelism and missions

_____ a prayer ministry composed of faithful saints interceding at all times

_____ a national TV/radio ministry featuring solid biblical exposition

_____ a top notch education program for children and youth

_____ a premier church-sponsored Christian school

_____ a biblical counseling ministry staffed by wise and godly leaders

_____ a vibrant inner-city outreach

Which "features" did you pick and why?

_____

_____

_____

_____

_____

_____

_____

Background of the Passage

Paul's letter to the Ephesians is concise in its language, yet comprehensive in its scope. This epistle is profound in its theology, yet practical in its application. In six brief chapters, Paul presents a logical and balanced view of all that's involved in knowing and serving the one true God.

As discussed in the last lesson, believers must remember that they are engaged in a cosmic, lifelong conflict. Satan does not give ground easily. He is a wily, dangerous foe, committed to the destruction of all his enemies. Thus we need armor and corporate, continual, and fervent prayer.

Ephesians begins by lifting us up to the heavenlies and ends by pulling us down to our knees. Paul focuses our attention fully on God and on our continued need for his help. God's armor is neither mechanical nor magical. We cannot simply take hold of it on our own and expect it to automatically perform supernatural feats. Our divine gifts—marvelous as they are—are impotent without the divine Giver.

In the closing verses of Ephesians, Paul gives general instructions about prayer, an illustration of prayer, and a closing benediction.

Bible Passage

Read 6:18–24, noting the key words and definitions to the right of the passage.

Ephesians 6:18–24

18 *praying always with all prayer and supplication in the Spirit, being watchful to this end with all perseverance and supplication for all the saints—*
19 *and for me, that utterance may be given to me, that I may open my mouth boldly to make known the mystery of the gospel,*
20 *for which I am an ambassador in chains; that in it I may speak boldly, as I ought to speak.*
21 *But that you also may know my affairs [and] how I am doing, Tychicus, a beloved brother and*

prayer (v. 18)—general requests of God

supplication (v. 18)—specific petitions

in the Spirit (v. 18)—in the name of Christ, consistent with His nature and will

being watchful (v. 18)—staying awake, being vigilant

faithful minister in the Lord, will make all things known to you;

22 whom I have sent to you for this very purpose, that you may know our affairs, and [that] he may comfort your hearts.

23 Peace to the brethren, and love with faith, from God the Father and the Lord Jesus Christ.

24 Grace [be] with all those who love our Lord Jesus Christ in sincerity. Amen.

that utterance may be given me (v. 19)—Paul's request is not for prayers for his personal well-being or physical comfort but for boldness to continue proclaiming the gospel, regardless of the cost.

ambassador (v. 20)—an envoy who represents a government

in chains (v. 20)—Paul wrote this letter while under Roman imprisonment.

Tychicus (v. 21)—See Acts 20:4–6; 2 Timothy 4:12; Titus 3:12.

comfort your hearts (v. 22)—literally "to call alongside" so as to bring encouragement

Understanding the Text

2) In this short passage, what does Paul teach about the variety of prayer? frequency of prayer? power and manner of prayer? objects of prayer?

_____

_____

_____

_____

_____

_____

3) Why doesn't Paul use this occasion to solicit prayer for his release?

_____

_____

_____

_____

_____

_____

(See 2 Timothy 2:9.)

4) How would you answer someone who argued that "praying in the Spirit" (v.18) means praying in an ecstatic language or "tongue"?

_____

_____

_____

_____

_____

_____

Cross-Reference

Luke 22:39–46 records the prayer vigil kept by our Savior in Gethsemane during His darkest hour. Consider how He braced Himself for the onslaught of Satan.

³⁹ Coming out, He went to the Mount of Olives, as He was accustomed, and His disciples also followed Him.

⁴⁰ When He came to the place, He said to them, "Pray that you may not enter into temptation."

⁴¹ And He was withdrawn from them about a stone's throw, and He knelt down and prayed,

⁴² saying, "Father, if it is Your will, take this cup away from Me; nevertheless not My will, but Yours, be done."

⁴³ Then an angel appeared to Him from heaven, strengthening Him.

⁴⁴ And being in agony, He prayed more earnestly. Then His sweat became like great drops of blood falling down to the ground.

⁴⁵ When He rose up from prayer, and had come to His disciples, He found them sleeping from sorrow.

⁴⁶ Then He said to them, "Why do you sleep? Rise and pray, lest you enter into temptation."

Exploring the Meaning

5) How does this passage contribute to your understanding of prayer as a weapon in our war against Satan?

_____

_____

_____

_____

_____

_____

6) Clearly, prayer is one of the critical components of Christianity; yet many believers seem to regard prayer as an occasional luxury. Why? How can we reverse this trend?

_____

_____

_____

_____

_____

_____

7) Read 1 Timothy 2:1–4. What insights do you learn for why Christians need to pray widely and continually?

_____

_____

_____

_____

_____

_____

Summing Up . . .

"In his *Pilgrim's Progress* John Bunyan tells of Christian's weapon called prayer, which, when everything else failed, would enable him to defeat the fiends in the valley of the shadow. Prayer is the closing theme of Ephesians, and though closely related to God's armor, it is not mentioned as part of it because it is much more than that. Prayer is not merely another godly weapon, as important as those weapons are. All the while that we are fighting in the girdle of truth, the breastplate of righteousness, the shoes of the gospel of peace, the shield of faith, the helmet of salvation, and the sword of the Spirit, we are to be in prayer. Prayer is the very spiritual air that the soldier of Christ breathes. It is the all-pervasive strategy in which warfare is fought.

"Jesus urged His disciples to pray always and not to lose heart (Luke 18:1). He knows that when the battle gets hard, soldiers easily become tired, weak, and discouraged. In the struggle with Satan, it is either pray or faint."
—John MacArthur

Reflecting on the Text

8) Through the centuries, Christian leaders have regarded prayer very highly.

"When God intends to bless His people, the first thing he does is to set them apraying."
Matthew Henry

"When we work, we work, but when we pray, God works."
Unknown

"A church without an intelligent, well-organized, and systematic prayer program is simply operating a religious treadmill."
Paul Billheimer

"The less I pray, the harder it gets; the more I pray, the better it goes."
Martin Luther

"Satan laughs at our toiling, mocks at our wisdom, but trembles when we pray."
Unknown

What do these quotes, and more important, the Scriptural texts studied in this lesson, teach or remind you as you contemplate your own habits of prayer?

_____

_____

_____

_____

_____

_____

9) Compare the content of Paul's prayers to the content of most prayers that you hear today. What is the difference?

_____

_____

_____

_____

_____

10) How specifically can you be more biblical in your prayer life this week?

_____

_____

_____

_____

_____

Recording Your Thoughts

_____
_____
_____
_____
_____
_____
_____
_____
_____
_____
_____
_____
_____
_____
_____
_____
_____
_____
_____
_____
_____
_____

For further study, see the following passages:

1 Samuel 12:23	Matthew 26:41	Luke 11:9
Luke 21:36	Acts 2:42	Acts 10:2
Romans 8:26–27	Romans 12:12	Philippians 4:6
1 Thessalonians 5:17		

Barbara — Praise for being @ Bible study again
Uncle in assisted living

Arlype — More time in prayer

Emily — husband in Europe for 3 weeks
safety, protection (Abbott)
protection for them while gone

Penny — Praise for school

Bessy — 2 kids — 10 yrs, 6 yrs
Can grow spiritually, and kids

Denise — 11 daughter   Praise, back again
9 sister   Petered out in the
6 daughter   past

Kawana — Jillian (granddaughter) — left
home for college   Santee → Chico
State
Safety, wise choices

Phuong — 1st gr - Joshua   Consistency in
preschool   coming to bible
study

Teri — 3rd gr - girl
1st - boy
long term   4 yr. old - preschool   Tentative about
care insurance.   bible study
Wisdom — where
kids shd. be

~~Jane~~ ~~When~~

Emily - Abbott - speaking engagement, headlin
speaker. 2 presentations

Organization - Use time well w. Abbott gov

Cisy - struggles - trip - "For the glory of God"
Husband - disagreement
respect from husband - left up
release   higher

Jane - Retreat
Praise -

Denise Cosgrove - ①Quiet time /Prayer time improve
in quality
②Understand - what God wants to do w. time
new. Act on it ③Mom's health - clear up
congestion (Wanda)

Arlype - Needs more time to pray - wants action
Sit quietly - 15 minutes morning

Kawana - Daughter in surgery - tendon in arm
(Dawn)   (help - out of work 6 mos.)
desperation - some improvement

Candace - Wisdom in dealing w.   14, 19, 12
Kids. Patience

Kawana - Brother-in-law had prostate cancer - (Richard)
    Might have a blockage in leg - ultrasound
Ultrasound on 14th
    Drs find out whats happening

Thong - tests for heart problems

Cissy - Praise

Arlyne - Daughter-in-law trying to adopt the
    triplets. Son (Praise

Terry - Jason "4yrs" has fever. Woke up a lot last
    night. Hernia possible

Laura - Praise

Penny - Fall Festival @ school went very well
    Nate's grades - College

June - Daniel

Emily - Abbott in Europe (2 weeks)

Denise - Sister-in-law — surgery tomorrow
    Worried about what they'll find
  Just having local anesthesia

    Jillian - no fever today
      is truly well

Penny - Nate's college app's - Grades getting better
    Nicole - decisions:

Arlyne - Have to let parents see them for
one hour/wk. until March. Friday
Son's box a strong Xian and prayed on phone - Carol
Lots of stress - Carol not a Xian.   & Kevin

Kowana - Granddaughter @ Chico, problems w.
roommate; She is angry w. best friend
Reconciliation

Cissy - Good dr. for back

Cheryl's husband - trip

Teri - Check-up tomorrow. Over cold/fever

Laura - Case (son) going thru divorce he
doesn't want since July
Accepted Christ in Alpha
Peace

Daniel - worth a try

June - flight to D.C.

Penny -